JIMMY GAROPPOLO

SUPERSTAR QUARTERBACK

BY TED COLEMAN

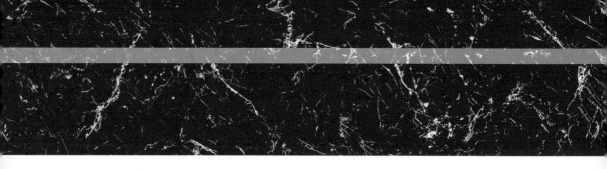

Copyright © 2021 by Press Room Editions. All rights reserved. No part of this book may be used or reproduced in any manner whatsoever, including internet usage, without written permission from the copyright owner, except in the case of brief quotations embodied in critical articles and reviews.

Book design by Jake Nordby
Cover design by Jake Slavik

Photographs ©: Joe Robbins/AP Images, cover, 1; Terrell Lloyd/AP Images, 4; Butch Dill/AP Images, 7; Nam Y. Huh/AP Images, 8, 20; Ken Trevarthan/Journal Gazette & Times-Courier/AP Images, 11; G. M. Andrews/AP Images, 13; Jason DeCrow/AP Images, 14; Peter Read Miller/AP Images, 17; Winslow Townson/AP Images, 19; Charlie Riedel/AP Images, 23; Marcio Jose Sanchez/AP Images, 25; Tony Avelar/AP Images, 26; Greg Trott/AP Images, 27; Red Line Editorial, 29; Gregory Payan/AP Images, 30

Press Box Books, an imprint of Press Room Editions.

Library of Congress Control Number: 2020901598

ISBN
978-1-63494-209-6 (library bound)
978-1-63494-227-0 (paperback)
978-1-63494-245-4 (epub)
978-1-63494-263-8 (hosted ebook)

Distributed by North Star Editions, Inc.
2297 Waters Drive
Mendota Heights, MN 55120
www.northstareditions.com

Printed in the United States of America
082020

About the Author

Ted Coleman is a sportswriter who lives in Louisville, Kentucky.

TABLE OF CONTENTS

1 MAKING A STATEMENT

Questions followed the San Francisco 49ers in 2019. They started the season red-hot, but were they really that good? And Jimmy Garoppolo was playing well, but was he really a star quarterback?

The player and the team both had a chance to prove it. The Niners faced the New Orleans Saints in Week 14. The teams had identical 10–2 records. Whoever won would have the best chance at earning home-field advantage in the National Football Conference (NFC) playoffs.

Jimmy Garoppolo was in command against the Saints in 2019.

Garoppolo had a huge game. He threw for 349 yards and four touchdowns. He matched legendary Saints quarterback Drew Brees in the shootout. The teams traded huge plays all day. Brees's fifth touchdown pass gave the Saints a 46–45 lead with one minute to go.

The 49ers tried to fight back. With 39 seconds left, they were on their own 33-yard line. It was fourth down. In tough situations, great quarterbacks look for their best playmaker. For Garoppolo, that was tight end George Kittle.

On fourth down, Garoppolo hit Kittle with a

STRONG PARTNERSHIP

George Kittle was Garoppolo's favorite target in 2019. He was the only 49ers receiver to be targeted 100 times. Kittle caught 85 of those passes for 1,053 yards and five touchdowns. The two are also great friends. After the 49ers clinched a trip to the Super Bowl, Kittle wore a t-shirt with Garoppolo's picture at a postgame press conference.

Garoppolo and Drew Brees, *left,* **chat after the shootout in the Superdome.**

perfect pass. Then Kittle kept going. He took the ball deep into Saints territory. The 49ers kicked a field goal to win the game. At 11-2, they had the best record in the NFC.

Garoppolo was named the NFC Offensive Player of the Week. There weren't many questions left about Garoppolo. However, one big one remained: how far could he take the 49ers?

2 ILLINOIS BOY

Jimmy Garoppolo came from a football family. His dad was an electrician, not a former star quarterback. But his older brothers Tony and Mike both played at Rolling Meadows High School in the Chicago suburbs.

Jimmy was born on November 2, 1991. When he got to high school, the coaches played him at linebacker and running back. He didn't switch to quarterback until his junior year. The starting quarterback got hurt, and Jimmy had to fill in.

Jimmy wasn't heavily recruited coming out of high school in suburban Chicago.

Jimmy ended up playing 19 games in his junior and senior seasons. He clearly could throw. He passed for 3,136 yards and threw 25 touchdown passes in two seasons. Those were good numbers. But they were not the kind of numbers that interested top college programs. And Jimmy had less experience at quarterback than most players.

Only a few colleges recruited Jimmy. And none of them were in the top division of college football. One was Eastern Illinois. Its coaches didn't think very much of Jimmy at first. But Jimmy's high school quarterbacks coach convinced them to take another look. They ended up offering Jimmy a scholarship.

Eastern Illinois had produced some great quarterbacks. One was Tony Romo, who played many years with the Dallas Cowboys

Eastern Illinois turned out to be a perfect fit for Jimmy.

in the National Football League (NFL). Jimmy saw Romo's name all over the record books. He wrote down all the records he wanted to break.

The Panthers were not a good team. They went 2–9 in each of Jimmy's first two seasons.

But he played well enough to earn the starting job just four games into his freshman year.

Things changed in 2012. Eastern Illinois hired Dino Babers as head coach. Babers ran an exciting offense that gave Jimmy lots of chances to throw. Jimmy threw for 1,200 more yards in 2012 than he did in 2011. He also threw 31 touchdown passes.

Jimmy was even better in 2013. In 14 games he threw for 5,050 yards and 53 touchdowns. He was just the second player ever at that level of college football to pass for 5,000 yards. Jimmy also broke many of Romo's school records.

WALTER PAYTON AWARD

Jimmy won an impressive award in his senior year. The Walter Payton Award goes to the best player in Jimmy's level of college football. Payton was a legendary running back for the Chicago Bears. Jimmy grew up a Bears fan. And Payton had lived in Jimmy's hometown of Arlington Heights.

NFL scouts got a good look at Jimmy when he played in the Senior Bowl at the end of his final college season.

It was hard to believe that few colleges had been interested in Jimmy four years earlier. Because now he was headed to the NFL.

3 THE BACKUP

Although Garoppolo came from a small college, many NFL teams were very interested in him. But the team that actually drafted him was a surprise. The New England Patriots already had a star quarterback in Tom Brady. But Brady was getting older. They took Garoppolo in the second round thinking maybe one day he could take over.

It was a great chance to learn behind a legend. But it also meant Garoppolo didn't see much action. Most of his playing time

Garoppolo was beaming after learning he'd been drafted by the Patriots.

came at the end of blowouts. Garoppolo made his debut in a Week 4 loss to Kansas City. He completed six of seven passes and threw his first career touchdown pass.

The next year, Garoppolo threw just four passes, but then he got his first real chance. Brady was suspended for the first four games of 2016. Nobody expected Garoppolo to be as good as Brady. However, he did a pretty good impression as he filled in for the all-time great.

Garoppolo made his first NFL start on September 11, 2016. The Patriots played the Arizona Cardinals on the road. It was under the lights for *Sunday Night Football.* After the Cardinals' opening drive stalled, the Patriots got the ball. It was Garoppolo's time.

He missed on his first pass. But he completed his next three to move the ball into

Garoppolo didn't seem intimidated when he made his first NFL start in 2016.

Cardinals territory. On second down, Garoppolo took the snap. He dropped back and saw wide receiver Chris Hogan streaking down the left sideline wide open. Garoppolo hit him perfectly with the pass for a touchdown. The Patriots went on to win.

The next week, Garoppolo threw three touchdown passes against Miami to build a 21–0 lead. But he didn't get a chance to finish it. A shoulder injury took him out of the game in the second quarter. Garoppolo wasn't able to make another start before Brady came back.

TWO RINGS

Despite mostly being a backup, Garoppolo won two Super Bowl rings while with the Patriots. The Patriots won the Super Bowl after the 2014 and 2016 seasons. In the second game, Garoppolo was the only member of the active roster who didn't play. The only playoff game Garoppolo played in was the 2014 conference championship.

Another chance at being a full-time starter would have to wait. Brady showed no signs of slowing down even as he turned 40. The Patriots started to think about trading Garoppolo. On October 30, 2017, they sent him to the 49ers in exchange for a 2018 second-round draft pick. Garoppolo's first chance

After spending three and a half seasons in Tom Brady's shadow, Garoppolo got his big break when he was traded to San Francisco.

to win a starting job in the NFL would come in

San Francisco.

4 JIMMY THE GREAT

The 49ers did not plan for Garoppolo to start right away. They had another young quarterback in C. J. Beathard who had been starting for them. Plus, San Francisco was off to an 0-8 start. There was no pressure for Garoppolo to rush in and save the season.

But Beathard got hurt near the end of a Week 12 loss to Seattle. Garoppolo came in and threw a touchdown pass on the game's final play. After that, 49ers head

Garoppolo got to face his hometown team in his first start with the Niners.

coach Kyle Shanahan named him the starter the rest of the year.

It was perfect timing for Garoppolo. The 49ers' next game was in Chicago against the Bears. Garoppolo had a lot of family and friends in the stands cheering for him. He threw for 293 yards and led a late scoring drive as the 49ers pulled out a 15-14 win.

Garoppolo provided a boost to the 49ers' offense. And the team went 5-0 with him starting. Garoppolo got rewarded with a new contract after the season. It was the biggest in NFL history at the time.

Garoppolo carried a 7-0 record as a starter into 2018. But his perfect record ended in Week 1. The Minnesota Vikings defense forced three interceptions. That was the most Garoppolo had thrown in a game.

A season-ending knee injury derailed Garoppolo in 2018.

But he bounced back. He threw two touchdown passes and no interceptions in each of his next two games. But he suffered a serious knee injury late in the Week 3 game at Kansas City. He missed the rest of the season.

Garoppolo was ready to go for 2019. He won his first start back 31–17 over Tampa Bay. In fact, Garoppolo and the Niners began the 2019 season 8–0.

The 49ers finished 13–3 and clinched home-field advantage throughout the playoffs. Garoppolo didn't do it alone. San Francisco had a strong running game and a great defense. In the NFC Championship Game, Garoppolo attempted only eight passes as the 49ers rushed for 285 yards against the Packers. The 37–20 victory gave the Niners a spot in the Super Bowl.

Facing the Kansas City Chiefs, Garoppolo and the 49ers built a 20–10 lead

PAYING THE PRICE

Garoppolo is not known as a troublemaker. His first fine came from just being too excited. After the 49ers beat Seattle to close the 2019 season, Garoppolo threw the game ball into the stands. The NFL considers this a safety issue and fined him $7,017.

Garoppolo celebrates the 49ers' trip to the Super Bowl.

early in the fourth quarter. But the Chiefs rallied for 21 points. The 49ers lost 31–20.

One loss could not erase the great season Garoppolo had. He had proven he deserved to start and could be a winner in the NFL. The next step in his career was winning a championship.

GO DEEP

In Week 16 of the 2019 season, the 49ers and Rams were tied with two minutes left to play. Jimmy Garoppolo led a game-winning drive that included two conversions on 3rd down and 16. On the second one, Garoppolo was rushed by four Rams. One almost hit his hand. But he stood tall and fired a 46-yard pass to Emmanuel Sanders. The 49ers kicked a last-second field goal and won 34–31.

TIMELINE

1. **Arlington Heights, Illinois (November 2, 1991)**
   Jimmy Garoppolo is born.

2. **Charleston, Illinois (2013)**
   Garoppolo throws for 5,050 yards and 53 touchdowns with the Eastern Illinois Panthers.

3. **New York, New York (May 9, 2014)**
   The New England Patriots select Garoppolo with the 62nd pick in the NFL Draft.

4. **Kansas City, Missouri (September 29, 2014)**
   Garoppolo plays in his first NFL game and throws his first career touchdown pass.

5. **Glendale, Arizona (September 11, 2016)**
   Garoppolo makes his first career start, leading the Patriots to a 23-21 win over the Arizona Cardinals.

6. **Santa Clara, California (November 26, 2017)**
   A month after being traded to San Francisco, Garoppolo plays in his first game for the 49ers.

7. **Chicago, Illinois (December 3, 2017)**
   Garoppolo makes his first start for the 49ers, beating his hometown Bears 15-14.

8. **Miami Gardens, Florida (February 2, 2020)**
   After leading the 49ers to a 13-3 record, Garoppolo plays in his first Super Bowl, but the 49ers lose 31-20.

MAP

Birth date: November 2, 1991

Birthplace: Arlington Heights, Illinois

Position: Quarterback

Throws: Right

Height: 6 feet 2 inches

Weight: 225 pounds

Current team: San Francisco 49ers (2017–)

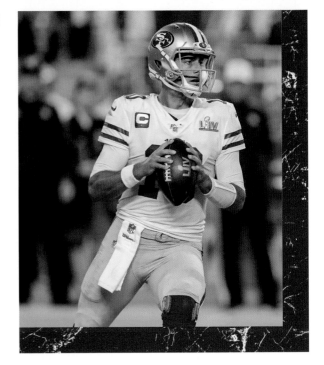

Past teams: Eastern Illinois Panthers (2010–13), New England Patriots (2014–17)

Major awards: Walter Payton Award (2013), Ohio Valley Conference Player of the Year (2013), Super Bowl champion (2014, 2016)

Accurate through the 2019 NFL season and playoffs.

GLOSSARY

blowout
Decided by a large margin; lopsided.

draft
A system that allows teams to acquire new players coming into a league.

drive
A series of plays in which one team has the ball.

freshman
A first-year student.

impression
An imitation of another person.

legendary
Generally regarded as one of the best to ever play.

playmakers
Talented players who often make game-changing plays.

recruit
Try to convince a high school player to attend a certain college, usually to play sports.

scholarship
Money awarded to a student to pay for education expenses.

shootout
A game that features lots of scoring and lead changes.

TO LEARN MORE

Books

Hunter, Tony. *San Francisco 49ers*. Minneapolis, MN: Abdo Publishing, 2020.

Whiting, Jim. *The Story of the New England Patriots*. Mankato, MN: Creative Education, 2019.

Whiting, Jim. *The Story of the San Francisco 49ers*. Mankato, MN: Creative Education, 2019.

Websites

Jimmy Garoppolo College Bio and Stats
www.eiupanthers.com/sports/football/roster/jimmy-garoppolo/3406

Jimmy Garoppolo Pro Stats
www.pro-football-reference.com/players/G/GaroJi00.htm

San Francisco 49ers
www.49ers.com

INDEX